Raw: poetry made from scratch

Latisha L. Ellis

DEDICATION

To the women of Dayton Correctional Institution,
the family I left behind
and the freedom that awaits them.
To Hyde for putting up with my BS and for typing this shit for me. Without
her, I'd be lying in a ditch somewhere with a torn notebook in my hand and
an inkless pen in the other.
And to the love of my life, I am thankful for the family you have given me.
You have made the bullet in my chest worth having.

Note: I would like to give thanks and much admiration to the great Vincent
van Gogh whose work I was allowed to use as the cover. He was a man in
love with his passion and bit mad, but aren't we all a little mad?

Introduction

Why must I think? Why am I not allowed the luxury to not feel? My heightened gift of insight has granted me the agonizing right to feel vulnerable. Weak. Defenseless. Exposed. Agreeing upon that it is needed to undergo such horrific sense of artistic pain. But I don't just want my poetry to be about pain, nor does it have to be about gender, sexuality, race or religion, but a taste into what is a giant palate of human emotions. Cultivating the generation that no longer in my mind appreciates poetry. But yet we have a wide range of art and expression that continually nurtures our society.

When people read my poetry, hear my spoken word, I want it to impact them. That this may not be Harlem, but a renaissance of words that express what it is exactly we need people to not know, but feel. Yes, feel. They do it in music; they do it through dance; they do it through painting, but there are some phenomenal poets out there. Dying to be heard. They are not just words, but emotional individuals that connect with you in a way you didn't know words could.

I find myself in awe at the stuff I read and beg for more. That in turn drives me to write, creating a chain reaction that open doors to other poets. Yes, poets. Anyone can write poetry, but it takes un-adulterated, self-exposing, brutal honesty with oneself to not just read between the lines but off the road into the desert past the skeleton with the scorpion crawling out of the eye socket. It smacks you like a comic book, "POW!" That makes you open your eyes and see the world not for what it is nor what it was, but what it will become. God is the greatest poet of all. You can hear God and Mother Nature speak every day. Those are the poems created by amazing poets that change me. Without poets, there would be no expression.

In the words of a poet I heard say as a child as I snuck and watched "Mos Def Poetry," they said: "Don't let your voice become a miscarriage; let your soul and tongue make love so it can give birth to expression!"

Quiet Room

Silent in the room, we sit back in our seats.
We do not speak, backs erect to steal glances, we do not dare.
Breathing questions, we ask in our quiet room.

They all know but we pretend.
As of right now, to her, I am a stranger,
a dark figure that represents a nasty taste in her mouth called
change.
For me, she is the unknown, a white swamp of the same muck
I have drowned in too many times before.

Clean slate.
We are each other's clean slate.
Washed clean of each other's past.
Shame no longer the odor that lingers from our pores.
Quietly, they all shout, SPEAK. But stubborn are we not?

I steal a look, boldly asking, "Why do you hate me?"
Her eyes reply subtly, "Because I hate myself."
Dropping her head in a stalemate, we go back to silence.
Only in our quiet room will she whisper to scream.

I Am From

I am from bikes laid out in the front yard while little bad ass kids
run around in the streets
where the air smells of cornbread and collard greens
where we walk by faith and not by sight
and a boy named Trey plays basketball all day and night.
I am from bullets spraying the ground like a rain shower
where supply and demand was weed, pills, and coke

where the only colors allowed in your crayon box was either red
or blue
and making it to 21 was too old to die too soon
I am from the only way to make it is dribble a ball, rap a line or
running track
when you turn around and there's a gun to your back
But I come also from strong black mothers raising their children
making ends meet
where mothers miss meals so us kids never went hungry
where they break fire hydrants as a way to cool off
and it was the dope dealers paying for formula and diapers and
bibs
where 50 cents got you a pop from the truck that sold ice cream
I am from where I am as you can see
I am who I am cause where I'm from made me

At the Starting Line

It was that simple
To point and pull the trigger
Dying is easy
Living is hard

But that's the best part
To live, I had to die
slow
Death was my head start

Well Spoken

I'm one of those special kids but not one of a kind. I was doing book reports on the Iliad and the Odyssey at the age of 9. And got $10 words that make like you were born to swing from vines. See, I have a well-spoken vernacular. They say, "You must hung with a lot of white people." Well, I guess you can say that, but the way I talk doesn't make me any less "black."

I grew up the same way where down the street the houses were used to trap and my cousin's kitchen was used by her boyfriend to cook up crack, when you turn on the lights all the roaches and rats just scat and on the 6 o'clock news some little girl was found dead in an alley out back.

Yeah, I hung with the white people, but I also kick it with the black folk. Where you step off the porch and all you got was hope. Kids choke on gun smoke and D-boys on the block selling heroin and coke and your best friend of today becomes tomorrow's new ghost. So just because I don't sound black doesn't change the fact that I still get stared at. Sorry if it's still hard to believe, say what you will but to them I'm still just some nigga that learned how to read.

Bliss

clouds cluster around me.

why is it so dark in here?

closed caption souls

whisper wisdom around me

biting my thumb to the sky

I question their words with a sneer

Fools, someone once said, fools such mortals be

rolling their eyes to such fruit of truth

they'd rather starve

than be subjected to the taste of knowledge

Substance

substance driving the impulse connection

to human and emotion

I feel when I am sober

I live when I am high

Rapid spurts of nonsense are injected

into their bloodstream

I feel when I am sober

I live when I am high

Bleak is their existence

Now

please let me close my eyes

Let the world fade and responsibility die

I'm not me when I am sober

I don't know you when I am high.

If my Bunkie was Langston Hughes

If my Bunkie was Langston Hughes, his pen would have a ball
So much his mind could say as it wanders from the ceiling to the
wall.
He would write about the little human part of us being ripped
away when CHOW TIME would be called. That's unless you act
like an animal, you get treated like a dog.
That the ones who are supposed to help you stand up are the
ones who stick their legs out for you to fall. That even in a
controlled environment, nothing's under control at all.
But he'll remain silent, and I'll pick up his perfect tool. He will
do nothing because there's nothing for him to do. For me with so
much to say and nothing left to lose, I'll stand up and speak
because my Bunkie is not Langston Hughes.

Angelic Death

Like broken wings on a butterfly
I've sat and watched an angel die
It didn't happen in a day, nor in a night
I had to watch and as tears filled my eyes, here's a thing you'll
wanna know
When an angel dies
she dies slow
And that once infinite glow she once showed
turns black as she decomposes
Her spirit shrivels and fills with holes
Her body stains her crown and robes
Her flesh peels and her eyes lay lifeless in her face
Her wings crack and stiffen from her fall from grace
She is a statue when she speaks
The chilling sound when an angel no longer breathes
I lost an angel along my way
now you know how an angel decays

Nice to meet you

A sweet suggestion of the hands is but a symphony orchestrated
by Cupid's bow.
The way she looks at me makes me rethink the image of myself.
A universal conversation, a love language I understand when
around her arms did fold.
I took a strand from Mother Earth's hair and under the stars I
knelt.
And in the garden of our Eden, I held my breath with eyes closed
When you said you were mine forever underneath Orion's belt
How simple is it to fall in love, how simple it is to fall right out.

I, for a second, question her answer 'til I heard this come from her mouth:
She said nothing for I have not met her yet because my heart is too clumsy.
I heard Mother Earth say, "Wait, my child, even bees take time to make honey."
'Til then, I'll wait patiently; dangling my feet in life's water.
Listening for the footsteps a tender stranger hearing my mother greet her and say,
"I would like you to meet my daughter."

En Garde

Crossing fingers
Sharpening swords
These are the wars
That we succumbed to
Gray smoke smothers the sky
Strangling from the constant fight of cries
Peace be still
From the destruction
There comes
peace

I Spy

Cautions. Looking. Spot.
    There she was.
Finding, holding, having.
    Here she is.
Warm, loving, caring
    She is mine.
Cold, chilly distant.
    She became.
Mute. Silent. Void.
Awkward silence when we're together.
Numb, emotionless, paralyze.
Her love no longer backed by anything.
Pushing, leaving, left.
    She is gone now.
Broken, shattered, smashed
    My heart.
Cautions. Looking. Searching.

They Call Her

In the valley of fire and ash, she is the gift left from God in
Pandora's Box.
The mother to the forgotten, the seeker to the absent.
The touch of her hand is but a warm breath on your skin.
Her smile welcomes hurt so she can begin the process of healing.
She is the mender of the damage.
The releaser of the shackle.
She forgives even when you haven't deserved it.

The lover of the loveless
She is the pallbearer of the living,
Guiding them from the river of Styx
For even the devil knows not to swear in her presence
She is the light to the sunless
She is knowns as faith
Some call her hope
God calls her peace
I call her Chelsie

Don't Be Alarmed

Cancerous.
A tumor growing inside the shell
of a man
Terminally
ill
from the grief and sheer exhaustion
of life
biting
swallowing nails
from the hands that feed him
polishing
shining the shoes
that trample all over him
every day

Choke
choking on the rancid
taste of what it was like to be free
Free
freed from the noise
freed from the consistent
bull
shit
of inconsistency
this
is only temporary
like Odyssey
fighting
escaping
death to be home
this
is only a test
nothing
more.
nothing
less

The Line Is Drawn; Do I Cross It?

What is my limit?
What boundaries do I cross when there is no longer a gray line to
separate good and evil?
Like exotic flowers, concentrated hate grows strong in its
greenhouse.
What am I living for?
A tug-of-war with man and God aiming to please the other.
We look back wondering when our debt is paid off so we can be
free like indentured servants.
I've lost myself along the way, time and time again.
Trying to mend what was never broken like ships lost at sea, I
become vacant and hopeless.
'Til one day I saw a lighthouse and you, guiding it.
Hand in hand, God and woman saving the soul I thought I had
lost a long time ago.
If pain were meant to be felt,
then love was meant to comfort it.

The Land of Broken Women

Sleep doesn't come to those who cry alone in the dark corners of
the room.
Greasy palms outstretch to grab someone's rusty heart.
Sheltering the chatter from the one that made them so fragile.
How can you save the hopeless?
How do you love the numb?
Healthy is unheard of, normal is forbidden.

Love is the supply, being needed is their demand.
Enslave them and they'll want you.
Love them and they'll mistreat it.
This is my world for now and in it,
nothing is worth keeping.

Lurk

Who are those they call monsters?
Ghouls of chaos that afflict panic
Devils of situation
Who am I to her that eat the flesh of solution?
Victim?
Prey?
An object of her sadist game?
No, I am the Casper of her heart
The specter of her mind
The shadow in the corner of her eye
The invisible presence that taunts her

She had love, but abused it.
She had wholeness, but abandoned.
She said I stalk her

Says I'm everywhere she goes
Watching her
Following her
Manifesting in the small areas of her life
She's right

I'll forevermore lurk in her midst
I am regret and she will never escape me

Utter

I mumble
I open my mouth and stutter
in an attempt to define and defend
who I am
speechless
am I
      wordless
      are my thoughts
how do I express and
explain
a stranger?
unknown person that I am
I remain
mute
loud can I be
but no sound
     SPEAK
          DEFEND
        TALK
            OPEN YOUR MOUTH!
Nothing.

Why?
because I have no idea where to start

judgment
can I speak judgments?
lines of characterization cast on me like
garbage
on prisoners being carried away
to death
that is what
I have become

a phrase
a syllable
a context to which I transcend
into a self-fulfilling prophecy
    MAD
my dear
that girl
has
gone   mad

Lessons To Be Learned

Right there. In the corner. Seduced.
    Over there. Against the wall. Taken.
        Down there. On the couch. I learned.
            Around there. Folded on the stairs. I practice.
She taught me seduction.

In there. My room. I felt her.
    Off there. By the school. I made her a woman.

Parked here. In my car. She did everything but give.
I taught her pleasures.

With her. In an empty apartment. She laid.
    Allowed her. On the carpet. To receive me.
I taught her control.

Over her. In her cell. I lecture.
    Beside her On her bunk. She shut me up.
        Underneath her. Against my skin. I learned.
           On top of me. Around my waist. She conquered
me.
She taught me love.

Maze for the Handicapped

Lukewarm asphalt, palms up, chest heavy.
Splitting copper pennies.
Praying I'm not just as lost as the other.
Solar concentration, breathe deep, breathe hard. Pain fixed with
masking tape.
Cuts open and spread wide like a Venus Fly Trap.
How brave are the coward's footsteps?
Not so quiet.
Not so subtle.
Peel back, expose.
Look.
Patience timid. Voice docile.
How crippling to lose yourself.
How crippling to never find it.

Winter's Duet

Snowflakes
Painted the ground its color
Innocent
Gentle is the word
When it is most
At peace
Hands clasped
By lover underneath the snow
Curtain trees
Crunch of fresh powder that echoes
The sound of children's
Laughter
Slush cold brings forth
Cups of warmth that savors cocoa
How delicious is Christmas with its mint
Green or its cherry flavor red mistletoes
Its flurries of calm
Peace on earth did the angels sing
Close your eyes and listen
As the snow
And earth
Harmonize

Trusting the Untrustworthy

Like newborns held in the arms of lost souls, where flowers
bloom in dark tombs under slabs of concrete, I've given trust to
those that live in anguish, feeding off black clouds of
resentment. Empty shell casings lay beside their feet gnawing on
the bones of the lesser. Scarlet skeletons crumble like fall leaves.

Their lungs working like exhausting pipes, filtering the toxins
they take in. they breathe out dust, shadowed by the fleeting
gloom of confinement. Tickled are they whom hurt the wretched.
Martyrizing the sweet selected few like myself.

Why do I give in to such hideous crucifixions to impalement of
the heart, the gruesome desecration of one's emotions? Easy. If I
didn't have pain...I would have nothing at all.
I've let myself become a victim
I enjoy punishment
Wasn't trust meant to be abused?

Push

Push.
I felt her push.
Don't close me out, I said. She did anyway.
She struggled building that wall she allowed me to demolish.
A roll of the eyes said leave, but the touch of her hand on my
shoulder, said wait.
I could challenge her; smell her lies and duel her to the ground.
Passive, I was to other, but her game of thorns did nothing. I let
go. She'd pull back. She wanted to crush me like the others. To

mean something to herself. That was her savory gratification.
How sadists feed. But indeed I was a masochist, just not hers.
It sickened her.

Shove.
Now she's in too deep. Swimming in emotions she has not felt in
forever
Or never. She had now realized she was drowning.
She shoves me away.
Don't close me out. No, I panic.
We're both screwed. I got close. I allowed her to get closer.

She loved it.
A business deal gone messy. A bond from screwing the balance
of friendship and other.
She was getting to me.
Dark versions of ourselves have emerged and we are not proud
of them.
But she's comfortable.
She enjoys it.

But the bond formed between heavy breathing and creating has
not been cremated. That's why I stay away.
No, not in fear of feelings fluttering back up, worst, allowing her
back in to finally finish what she started because the distance
was betrayed.
To make me another corpse in her garden of decaying hearts.
She craves it.

Feel

Touching the emptiness of life, I grasp and take hold of its meaning. "Cut me," the world said. Mother Earth gives me her arm and I plunge my razor into her. She exposes herself. I breathe in dirt and ash. Clay and mud. What humans taste like as I stick out my tongue and sip. She cradles me, as I lap up the rest of the spillage onto the universe.
Now I am alone, hostage of my own conclusion of love. An on-looker it is. Merely a spectator to life. Indulging in its own game of insanity. I asked for a chance and love did spit in my face. Its saliva tastes like pain. Answers that belong to no questions. Blinded by its cape of content. I no longer wish to feel. I asked Mother Earth what is the point of pain? She said, "It lets you know you're still human."

Crenshaw

Street lights and cigar smoke
What do you want from me, Crenshaw man?
White chalk lines
And black coats
Silence and motions
For my hand
Yellow tape and blue suits
Where are we going, Crenshaw man?
Crying women and black boots
"Don't worry," he says, "You'll soon understand."
White sheet
Missing shoe

Where, please, where, Crenshaw man?
Black arm
My tattoo
"Onto Heaven
That's the plan"

Distances

She keeps me within her circumference, distance is our silent
treaty. I dwell on the outskirts of her world so not to disturb the
ghosts of intimacy that follows us like John Does in trench coats
at night. She keeps me at bay; it keeps her safe. How terrified
she must be to walk on eggshells quietly praying not to resurrect
the feeling that lay dormant in the back of her head.
Once a figure, I open my skull and pour my thoughts and
ambitions into her parched throat that I am now a sensation. A
feeling that sends pleasure and peace through her blood vessels.
She hated it.
We indulge ourselves within safe limits until she had to laugh.
She laughs. She laughed because it was no longer distant. She'd
lay her face in my neck and listen to the fanatical, altruistic
things ooze from my tongue. In my arms did this depress
postmortem world disappear. She felt secure.
She despised it.
She spoke and I listened. No, I wasn't the one from her past but
his phantom hovered over me. I listened. That's what made me
different from the others. I understood. Bound in her constraint,
locked in her cage, the small still voice crying out to be heard, I
reached and my hand stuck out in the dark like a lantern telling
her it's okay. You are not alone. She was protected.

She loathed it.

Space. Space was no longer a problem. That was the issue. She wasn't cheap. In the eyes of mine, she knew her worth. She was priceless—a trail of hearts painted her history. But I wasn't one of them. She couldn't break me and yet all the worry that I could break her.

She detested it.

Klansmen

My momma taught me to hold
my tongue
Whenever
I speak
She said speaking my mind would cause
them to creep
They came in the night
trust and believe
The creepy crawlers come out of the dark dressed
in white sheets
They came and got my daddy
while he was asleep
They drug my daddy out of bed and strung him
 in the trees
Creepy crawlers got my daddy
I hear his body swinging in the breeze
I'll stay quiet
Praying the creepy crawlers don't
Catch me

Tripping on E

Dreams, like camouflaged shadows dancing upon wicked
facades that mask the mind's intellect
Coded shapes sliding back and forth like wheels on a train
working speeding forward because it cannot go back.
Crazy is the mind that weeps for prosperity.
Demons chasers dress as angels confiding in secret chambers of
the common.
Plastic cigarettes lie like blanks in skulls of the "not needed."
Held in the palms of crustaceans that crawl around the world in
search of wise copper instead of fool's gold.
Quickly scattering the footprints of the ones who witness the
massacre of silence.
Appalled are the kings of this world that they may fall victim to
this conquest of hatred,
self-absorbed pit of faulting wiring.
Mouth dry, opens wide to drink the rain only to find the rancid
taste of Mother Nature.
I was merely asleep for all of this, so may I ask what are you
tripping on?

Wait

Comfort me.
I reach out with long, somber arms
Praying for somebody to reach back
As I wait
My mind fades into a gallery of inconsolable spirits looking for a
way home
Come to me.
Scared to cross another substance that can cause me harm that I
fear to grab love for it might retract
Take a break

I hear my heart say because
Love is a mortal verb
Of control
Strength that dares to be alone

Sour is rejection that makes my stomach curdle
How shabby contempt can be that it spares suitors egos
Because it knows how swift their hearts can be
Simultaneously changed

Love stares at its reflection
Leaving me black and purple
It's friends, Misery and Agony, tear me to seams
Breaking me down with Newton's Law
I scream
"LOVE is coming for me!
You'll see!"
And they just smile and say,
"Funny,
I know Love and
Love doesn't know your name."

Geo Techno

We are a generation that fuels frustration belittled by our own
ignorance
Suffocating damn near waiting on our significant replacements
Pounded by self-righteous bigots opposed to the art of self-
expression
A dying breed have we become

Molding our minds like Play-Doh, doing what the government
says
Playing the game because Uncle Sam says so

Victims to this co-culture of intellectual scum
That rather texts "hello" to their kids at the dinner table
A vicious cycle are we of Darwinism
But what are we to do when Darwin's cycle of the lesser has
become the whole generation?

Preservation of a less than temptation that screams conversation
but wiped out by the latest technology
That rapes pure communication of one's mind, body and soul
That personal contact has now been split into a form of
segregation that you must ask yourself
When was the last time you talked to someone that caused you to
use the cords in your throat to vibrate?
And your brain to produce words to a special person on the
phone? Mail?
When was the last time you turned the page of a book that didn't
mean swiping the screen?

On my conquest to understand this comatose victims of press
dying from the disease that oppresses the creative mind that
comes from the virus that infects our lives on a day-to-day basis
Trying to accept this new line of less in my eyes except realize I
can't face it
Sadly I have no longer the patience for our own benign
innovations that turn our soon-to-be brain-dead generations to
meat puppets

So put down the screen, is all I'm saying, and let the renaissance
of intuitive minds resurrect our generation

Black Bones

They say the white people made me
who I am
By the way I talk and behave
The voice of a house nigga
The skin of a field slave

Say what they will
But in my heart it
Beats of a drum from home
White words
Dark skin
Cut deep
And you'll find
Black bone

My complexion is only
A reflection of those who made these bones
Legislation plus segregation
Conceives white only zones
Emit Till beaten
Thrown in a lake
For winking at a China white doll
From King and Medgar Evers
To Little Rock
Deep in the heart of Arkansas

Tubman, Parks and Angelou
Set the tone
The power deep in black women
Built from black bones
Generations of dark skinned people
That instead became renegades
Social anarchy of democratic hypocrisy

Skin from the color of caramel to skin the color of
Smooth coal
From the pirates we learned English
To transform into our own secret code
Like "cool cat" to "jive turkey" to
"homie"
A rich dialect of chocolate lingo
From black paint to black fist raised high
At the Olympics drape
Around afros wearing black gold

All these people paid the way
So our lives no longer had a toll
Lives lost
Paid the cost
No, not with their souls
But for me to be free
As you can see
Was paid with
Black bones

Tick. Tick. Tick. Tock

Time locked like a passerby
Time shocked like the naked eye
Tick tock tick tock oh how the fun never stops
Time brought by the rich
Time taken from the sick
Time short for the ones that live quick
Timeout for those that don't keep guns at their hips
Tick tock tick tock oh how the clock goes
Tick tock tick tock
The only thing that it doesn't do is go
Slow

Does Your ID Badge Have A Number?

Oh, how the coin soldiers march in place
They walk with shiny boots of malice and disgrace
Oh, the tiny soldiers as they grimace with their catchers at such
distaste
All but numbers, bodies shaped as digits with no face
Toy soldiers telling me I am ward of the State
Unknowing that they themselves are property too
They eat the same food, just off prettier plates

Invitation Only

Stern truth accompanied by its elegant lie as they dance off my
tongue out of my mouth.
To wash away my sins only means I am covered in inequity.
My trespasses are wrongs made against myself.

Blame everyone.
Shame no one.

I dish out sorry's left to right because it's easier to apologize
than to remain silent.

Everyone wants to cradle a sorry.
No one wants to shelter a scream.

A project boarded up for lack of creativity because I've been too
preoccupied to face the stiff, cold eyes of the truth
And instead flirting with its guests.

Lying to yourself is easy
It's telling yourself the truth that's difficult.
My, my, Self-pity, what a lovely party you've thrown.

Remedy

Her taste was their destruction
But mine
Was of peace
Her taste brought me back from the dead
To them were they
Deceased
From her cup did I sip
Slow
My joy and sweet release
From her cup did they find it bitter and with Hell heat
I found truth
And life in the bottom of her cup
They found helpless, crippling with a crutch
Beaten
Sliced
Torn
We all had lain
And she offered us a drink
For me it made me
Stronger
While the other laid and wasted
Condemn were they all when they took a sip
Her elixir for me gave sweet words that
Soften my lips
From her goblet did my pain cease forevermore
She was their poison
She is my cure

And They Want Me To Plead The Fifth!

FREEDOM WRITERS! FREEDOM WRITERS! CRY OUT
FREEDOM!
Like barbed wire claws grip on the shoulders of the oppressed
Bleeding from the cortex, they shout, "Treason!"
How dare they rip away the clothes of the first amendment and
VIOLATE!
A land of liberty and our freedom and the pursuit of happiness?
The pursuit torn away like Jewish books burnt in propaganda
fires.
        Our colors of the flag representing the ever-growing
pilgrimage pride? No!
But colors representing of the bodies sowed to reap the land of
the free
RED liquid smear over the flesh of yellow, red, and dark babies
WHITE snow to cover and wash away the decomposing stench
of people being stripped away of their homes
BLUE frostbite fingers of the hands of the natives walking the
Trail of Tears, homeless and scatter. No longer humans but
mascots like *The Redskins*.
        We talk about "Remember the Alamo."
Oh, I remember a fight over a land that wasn't ours to begin
with. We yell and protest and call them the "illegal aliens" when
we are the ones that invaded.
That they don't belong when 2/3 of this land was theirs to begin
with. But strangers like news kids on the playground kicking
people of the slide proclaiming that this is now our when they
were willing to share. Liars of democracy. Murders of the
freedom cry.

I am WRONG for what I am writing because I am RIGHT!
They are preaching history glories, not its slaughter house rise to
success.
Black skin whipped white. Red skin turns blue.
I write the wrongs because they promised forty acres and a mule.

To shut the truth from our mouths.
From our hands.
From the lead and ink we once bled.

Night and Day

from the Insider:

Soapbox cars mesh together like subway trains in underground

tubes of material solids

they chase laughing at the noise as it swindles

the street of its space to be young simply means to not be old

the light post flickers

the alley cats venture off

the world is our playground but we're too big to play on the

jungle gym

a world meant for living beings

I'm no longer a living being but a digit

a numerical value

captives of our world, chained to fences,

they stare at us

do they see animals or reflections of oneself?

they rule with the fist of a bully-child seeking vengeance upon

those who wrong them

a marvel world seen through glass eyes

from the Outsider:

But after a generation of gray, a slit appears in the melancholy

mist

a spark glances with God-given eyes

I wink

it winks back blocking the view of the knuckles

the mirror echoes majesty

I see daffodils and green meadows and sun beams

the tree swing within reach and I hear my name

a shadowy figure blocks my vision

my heart shivers falling yet again and quick as lightening in the

void,

my name, like Mom used to say

golden labs and bluebirds congregate

my laugh bubbles into my ear without thought

I fall prostrate in the waving wheat and the clouds swirl like

finger-paint

Smoke Break

A Black 'n Mile hangs out over the tip of my tongue.
I am temporarily numb transfixed by the smoke.
I hear the pitter patter of freelance raindrops hit the top of the car.
I close my eyes, I don't even remember driving.
The clouds squeeze water onto me, washing off conviction.
Rinsing me of confinement, I open my eyes.
My cigarillo dry as the desert burns like tinder.
The world and I are clean.
In the distance, I hear someone say, "Why is she just sitting on a car smoking in the rain?"
I smile to myself.
I guess they've never been to prison.

ABOUT THE AUTHOR

Always drawn to poetry and literature, Latisha L. Ellis discovered her passion while incarcerated. With her time, she created the contents of Raw. She was born in Baltimore, MD and moved to Columbus, OH when she was five years old. She grew up loving *Dragonball Z* and reading books like the *Odyssey* and *The Iliad,* trying her best to fit in. Then she realized she was a pretty damn cool, black kid. She learned that kindness breeds kindness and you should choose kind over being right. She has been published in The Clarion and also Mock Turtle Zine.

Made in the USA
Monee, IL
04 April 2022